Shrines of
Upper Austria

PHOEBE POWER received an Eric Gregory Award from the Society of Authors in 2012 and a Northern Writers' Award in 2014. Her poems have been published in journals and anthologies including *The Rialto*, *Oxford Poetry* and *The White Review*. She has recently collaborated with other artists on projects including a live performance of her pamphlet *Harp Duet* (Eyewear, 2016), and *Christl*, a video installation involving poetry, visual art and sound. She currently lives in York.

First published in Great Britain in 2018 by
CARCANET PRESS Ltd
Alliance House, 30 Cross Street
Manchester M2 7AQ

A CIP record for this book is available
from the British Library, ISBN 9781784105341.

Design: Luke Allan.
Printed and bound in England by SRP Ltd.

The publisher acknowledges financial assistance
from Arts Council England.

Acknowledgement is made to the editors of the
following publications, where some of these pieces first appeared:
The White Review, *The Quietus* and *Oxford Poetry*.

Shrines
of Upper
Austria

Phoebe
Power

CARCANET

for my family

Contents

sex and love with the soon-to-be accountant   9
what young india wants   10
Rina   11
The Moving Swan   12
children   14

★

Epiphany Night   17
Austrian Murder Case   18
Ice Rink   25
from A Tour of Shrines of Upper Austria   26
fasching   30
Installation for a New Baby   31
Goat Grave   32
8th May   33
Isis and Marija   34
Georgiana   35
Production Line of a Small Gift for the Ladies   36
Puppet-Maker   37

★

Name   41
Es war einmal   42
now I'm a bit mad   43
Villach   44
I wish she'd never told me   45
Schloss Cumberland   46
there was this fellow   48
1943–5 Ebensee   49
you don't know what's true   50

In and Out of Europe   51
I'm not coming to a country   52

★

notes on climate change   55
silver white winters that melt into springs   58
Eisblumen   60
the weather's changing   61
then you boil the milk   62
Milk   63
lovely sausages   64
British   66
some people have tea   67
Austrian pastorals   68
somewhere   69

Glossary   71

*Shrines
of Upper
Austria*

sex and love with the soon-to-be accountant

REFLECTIONS: TO RELY ON IN HIS NEW JOB

sets of suits and clear
surfaces, pairs of socks in black
and black, vehicular ease, swivel
chairs, wrapped
sandwiches and selfies secure
and hairless, you may be sure of it,
card's slide out,
regular payment, her legs on screens
duplicated
you look good in black and white

WEAPONS: WITH WHICH SHE THREATENS HIM

her tongue, kissing him all over,
hands on his lovely long hands, his own
beautiful hands hurt him, her purple-coloured
self that goes and grows

with this mirrored body
I just find you attractive

get the payment, slide the card in,
black lingerie and – depend on it –
bronzer, no hair, wrapped
sandwich, swivel chair, socks,
suit, surface. She's gone.
No picture to play;
wiped memory.

what young india wants

money: the unauthorised
biography, mad money
adventure, how you can learn
from apple and make money.
the seven secrets
of leadership, how google works, think
big: be positive and brave
to achieve your dreams
                      < ask not
for money, but for lakshmi >

Rina

She used to faint, her hair
        flapping beside her, eyes
spinning back through her head.
        She grew an eating disorder like
a germ in a test tube, or a baby.
                Never said what was in her
soul, but left her pink lips
        prissed forward at us, to guard her.
Then she got thinner, till she was a slick
                question mark in a long dress.
At every stage, the pattern in her face
                        faded more.

I saw her on the arm
        of a train operator. He was all
apologies and watches. Eventually
        she drew up a chair at the office herself
and went to work. She never missed a day.
                        Then a shadow
drew down behind her eye.
She woke one Monday, and could not see
                through both her eyes.
They said
        a shadow has drawn down
behind this eye.
                I saw her the next week at a party.
She didn't mention it.
        Her eyes were just as big,
                and bare, and blue as I remembered.

The Moving Swan

There were candles at the bottom of the
cathedral. They floated in a round pool,
on a trestle made of thin legs of iron. The
candle flames were soft and mobile, made
from water. They moved around the trestle-
top in a circular motion.

She held the drops of motion in her eye.
They were the only live thing in the cathe-
dral. The candles told her:

INTERLUDE: A DREAM

About a year after this happened I dreamed I was on a set of flying
swings, the kind you get on carousels at fairs. Only these swings
were high up on a mountainside, and you had to have a ticket, and
it was thronging. We pushed forward with our strips of tickets and
grabbed a swing before they rose up and away. A strong fairground
guy was there to help people onto the swings. I had one next to
Joanna. We were lifted into air, with nothing above below or to the
right or left of us.

We spun down and saw the green and cream landscape and riv-
ers turn beneath us. We talked about Mike. I asked Joanna if she
thought he thought I was too serious. Seriousness can be a great
asset, she said.

We dropped lower, into the city now, called Vienna. The lanes were
cobbled and narrow; the tops of our heads skimmed the low arches
as we sailed by. Then I caught sight of the back of a bullet-head I
recognised, walking in the direction away from us. It was ——

When we'd gathered down on the platform ready to unbelt and get down from the swings, the bullet-head was there again, and stalked up to me. He put his hand under my T-shirt and tried to stroke my lower back.

Get the fuck off!
I said hey look. Can't we be friends?

children

after Egon Schiele: Stadtende

sheen and clank
snakes to this colour town
this shout! and noise –

those letterboxes squeezed
to points – faces raised
to roofs! crammed

aqua violet orange
– figures getting down
from window frames

swung open –
raised arms and bended –
scarlet and yellow trousers!

children running
verging the dark
world of tree and linelessness

calling from the roofs
and from the giant
leaves – dark green!

Epiphany Night

bells outside my wohnung
tungatungatungatung!
men in tall white hats
make a ring
hats with paper fringes
men in long white robes

then the kings
come by boat
cross the See
from dark mountains.

comes the boat
crossing dark water.

step down drei könige
in fancy robe and blackface paint

then they come with lanterns
pointing orange yellow white
pointing lantern hats then start to
multiply in all directions, starshapes,
lanterns carried everywhere
bobbing like a lake

then all the handbells stop
and ring as one
tungatungatungatungatung!
behind the See
washes at our backs

Austrian Murder Case

AT THE KONDITOREI

Close, warm, and humming with the relaxed sounds of post-mid-day Kaffee-Kuchen. The cakes are modestly presented in a glass cabinet: stripes of sponge alternate with chocolate cream; globes of mango gleam on mousse. Oblongs of raspberry and banana jelly. Older couples sit at round tables, sip kaffee and lift cake-cream inch by inch to mouths. They're conscious not to eat too quickly, so as to avoid nausea, and ensure instead continued pure delight. A little nothing, pleasant chat; a few read the papers.

Our protagonist has the table by the window, hung with a doily curtain. There's a cigarette smoking itself out in his thrown-away left hand; his closed right one rests on the open pages of an empty notepad.

SEE (1)

Florian was walking with his schnauzer, Bernie, along the far shore of the See. He preferred this less trodden, further side because it meant he had a good view of the town, busy and self-important on that nearer side. And he liked being closer to the great faces of mountains, which jacked themselves right up hard, grey and granular, above all the people's things and houses.

His head was clear and only had in it air, Bernie running and her fetching the next stick, and the soft-firm earth and grass under their feet.

They stopped on the path to look over the See. Its surface was soft as a lady's undergarment. You could place your finger in and feel it drop under, without resistance. Today's winter water had black, mirrored surfaces; nothing could be seen beneath them.

Then Florian's eye settles on something, as a fisherman focuses on the red point at the end of his line in the water. His eyes are drawing an outline – round the objects he can see. They are – this shape – like this – two rectangles bobbing among some dead black stalks. The black of the rectangles is greyer than the See's black. Their sheen is harder than the water's; more moulded, less easy to penetrate.

The protagonist arrives at the pension. This is situated in the village adjoining the town, where slopes are levelled in tiers to make space for the houses. There are broad, roofed shelters to store rows of clean logs for heating the farmhouses.

As he completes his information in the hotel ledger on the counter, something catches his eye. He pauses. Another guest is in the doorway, dragging two large, grey plastic cases. They must be very heavy, judging by the discomfort of the man dragging them indoors, the sweat on his brow and the red of his face.

'Hallo Herr Leitner,' says the pension owner, over the shoulder of the protagonist bent over the ledger. The handles of the suitcases spring back into place as the guest lets them go to return to his car. The pension owner explains to the protagonist that Herr Leitner holidays here in the village by the See every year. Usually he would bring his wife. By the look of the luggage it would appear that she is joining him later. The Herr had made a last-minute reservation for the New Year; perhaps it is a surprise occasion for her, the pension owner suggests, and he is going to fetch her subsequently, with everything made ready for her here first. That wouldn't be rather strange – to make a preliminary trip only for the luggage? The owner laughs at the foreigner. 'No, not really strange.' Herr Leitner reappears heaving a third piece, a woman's black, faux-leather holdall with patent panels.

HANDS AND FEET

Bernie is excited by the smell in the suitcases. They are heavy, and Florian is curious too. He prises open the slimy rim of one of the cases. Inside, right there on the lake path: somebody's feet and hands, cut off.

THE DIVERS

The police fitted the masks over their faces, oxygen tanks securely clipped. The superintendent watched while his men slipped into the water, as easily as steel poles or two long fish. The See closed after their entrance her soft, wide black eyelid.

They weren't long gone. This was the sixth dive. They had already found a male corpse, so the superintendent was pleased. But the last diver believed he could make out a second shape between the rocks on the lake-bed here – 5 KM out in the water and 150 M deep – something artificial, but he needed assistance to dredge it out.

The superintendent watched as the two divers re-emerged. At first, only the neoprene tops of their heads were visible, like the caps of mushrooms. Then their plastic eyes, followed by the whole hi-tech, life-saving contraption of gear rigged on their narrow shoulders. The divers staggered over the reinforced deck of the police boat, dragging between them a black bag, veined with green and water: a dank-smelling women's holdall.

HEAD

Just the head itself. Oblong of blue-cloud
concrete – cheap, breeze-block type – piled
round the damp ovoid of face and eyes.
Head + Block. hedinblok. Sculptural; a
possible art piece?

Her, cast. What could you do with the
concrete shell of her? Make another her.
In fibreglass, beeswax, plaster, bronze.
But this cast is poorly made. Inside, the
head of her's too heavy, weighs its inner
jellies down to burst the tensure of the
sand and stone grains which surround her.
The concrete barely reaches her cheeks,
lips, eyebrows, nose in patches. There are
fragile rings of grey and silver hair. The
head-matter, blood and damp, sags of
skin – strains against this brutal box.

Nose tilts up, the forehead raised. Maybe she's an angel zephyr
made from chiselled stone, her eyelids flowing lines of wind. She
rides up mountains – out of box, suitcase, coffin, block.

SEE (2)

The See looks on. The protagonist walks away, notepad in hand. He leaves the town with his insight into one dramatic story, like the brief, quivering shudder of a swimmer as she leaves the lake, feels the air on body, cold.

The See looks on. She looks at herself. Because she is the See she can begin to see from the perspective of her liquid centre, her navel, and see all the shores as equidistant from this point. In all directions is only sleek black water, the houses distant rectangles.

See swallowed the man and his body, the plastic bodies of his cases, the contents / bodies of the hands and feet of his dismembered wife. See swallowed him and his ball and chain: the heavy block of head with its agonised face, heaved beside him in a black holdall. The failed sculpture all cast and ripped, dead biological matter straining its manmade case.

The lake swallowed it all, feeling green and secret. But still they scanned and fished. They plumbed a line and got all the things out, laying them one by one on the deck, and fitted them together in their human way, to get to the bottom of the story.

Ice Rink

slippery translucent globe
lit pink, or blue, or light green.
cutting through the top

like milk or foil or egg or skin
and sliding on parallel lines, then
crisp surface, ridges raised.

plastic-covered blades. beat:
synthetic girl's voice
pops around this indoor space.

friends hold hands; littlies
shuffle in their spacesuits
hanging on to penguins;

parents loosely dance behind.
this jolly light world
of flying and seeing;

the jolly bright world

from A Tour of Shrines of Upper Austria

STOP I: ECK I

two perspex jars of candles:
egg pool of wax, yellow flame
burns through lent, anticipating easter.

windowbox of deep pink
primrose, and spiking bulbs
white, moving up to green.

behind, the painting:
mary gets a crown, ascension.
seven stars of straw
tucked in the top iron frame.

first I'll draw,
then photograph.

if you wanted you could stay
till the flame burned down.

I have to kneel
inside to take a good picture

STOP 2: ECK 4

space inside for six
on curvy pews of pine
pots of lip-red heather
and the usual heart portraits
fingers pointed at chests

STOP 3: ECK 9

this one's for mothers,
all dead and dying mothers.

mary's in a frame there
her dress pulled back to show
her grey and red heart
pierced with a knife and lilies.

jesus too with his bared heart.
and a monk holding a baby
on his arm like a father.

in a frame's a worried mother
kissing the hand of a child in bed.

and a sewn tea-cloth, black thread
on grey-white linen:
Wenn du noch eine Mutter hast,
Danke Gott und sei zufrieden,
Nicht jeden auf der Erderund
Ist dieses höhe Glück beschieden.

STOP 4: INTERNAT (EINTRITT VERBOTEN!)

bunch of woollen flowers
    scarlet and ocean blue
    heap of pine and pine cones
dusty old frame with a prince inside

STOP 8: LITTLE MARY

calm to be here mary
mary in grey plaster
figure with a basket crown

christmas branches round her
deep pink and white
heather at her feet

and long fine strands
of wheat with soft ends
tied with a ribbon

mary and jesus stand in the window
frame all white flaked paint
blue and grey relief

STOP 9: ON THE CORNER OF FRIEDRICH-HEBBEL STRAßE AND PEPÖCHSTRAßE

brown-stained wood
like a hut or shed,
carved roof hood.

heraldic, coats of arms
and initials:

E.T.L.   O.U.E.T.   M.H.T.

inside, dungy.
among things
somebody's cross-stitch:
St Franzisha.

STOP 13: KROTTENSEESTRAßE

christ out of spikes
or virgin fanned by tongs,
gold-brown teeth and hairgrips

fasching

at Elli's schmankerlstube it's all
drinking and bosners.

in neukirchen it's ten a.m. and children are dancing in a pen. They're
dalmatians, indianers, cowboys with foamstick horses and goggle
eyes. Two headteachers smile and joggle in a pair, her cruella fish-
net makeup and his penguin suit, peaked beak. High loud music
wrenches in the outdoor light, rips fabric. Dance the children on.

A multicoloured snake or train of people tooting its bells and flute,
curving down the road beneath the green banks and a big sky, the
mountains.

Installation for a New Baby

HANNA LENA
29.02.2016
4285 g
51 cm

To celebrate the Hanna Lena we cut storks
from hardboard, painted white
with black outlines, orange legs and disney eyes.
We tie balloons from oberbank and peg a row
of weeny clothes, jeans and 'gros, nine
still-folded size 1 nappies, marked
each with a letter of her name.

We save soup cans, bean and veg tins
to clatter where they trail the grass,
pin a spray of rubber dummies and a
pillow, sagging rain. The doll of her
sits forward in a car seat, up-raised
polyvinyl queen. *Na ja*, we marker-pen,
was kann es schöneres geben
als ein kleines neues Leben?

Goat Grave

collocation of yellow
easter pansies and soft willow
hardboard sprayed magenta
RIP   BART

two heaps of ivy / straw
one unlit red tealight –
two goats died, one
piebald, one brown.

made-up shrine, installation;
cartoon **BART**

goat parents sit aside:
homer, marge.

8th May

bells are ringing, there's a fire
sailboats calmly over the lake

berufsschule kids smoking cigarettes
dropped a spark in a dried-up rose
which travelled up the vine and took
the whole of the roof in flames!

Ebenzweier is burning!
people gathered to watch the smoke
pummelling the sky,
the definite orange lay waste
and the flaccid jets of the hoses

people were crying!
at the loss of the building

Isis and Marija

Isis doesn't like that her name sounds like
the terrorist group   Isis
from Colombia speaks Espagñol
will not 15 cause she will Peter Pan
the only girl in soft grey sweatpants
in the art class brushes
a waveshape, blue-violet-green
while the other kids draw in pencil first
a fish, a plant, a boat

Marija loves Isis; Marija needs friends, she dominates a friendship.
Let's go shopping! Isis is so funny girl. Both don't speak so good
german but are good in english, and understand all

★

Marija: at this school I don't learn anything! They just give us work
and we don't must do it. In my last school the teacher stand at the
front we take notes we learn something. My mother come first from
Croatia for one year. Then we all come. I live in a hotel, five minutes.
I don't like live in the hotel because I don't can see my friends in my
house. Isis has next week a party, pyjama party. We play games, talk,
maybe go shopping, I don't know. It's really good.

Georgiana

20, cackle bright as a thin tree opening,
diagonal, energy-black eyebrows.
Hair black-amber, lipstick,
cigarette pack, phone.
Her boyfriend here's Romanian,
does the housework, she's from Puglia,
works 3 or 4 jobs cleaning houses.
20 aunts live here 15 years
so she sets up, gets the car,
takes German class and speaks
fast with a curly accent she won't change.
She made today polenta, schweinfleisch
and a salad, and does fitness.

Production Line of a Small
Gift for the Ladies

While she scissor-curls the ribbon
Sara knots the cellophane.

While she tightens cellophane
Eleni cuts the ribbon up.

While she snips the ribbon lengths
Frau G. bunches up the cellophane.

While she scrunches cellophane
Isis lays the shells on sand.

While she organises shells
Lucas sprinkles sand on glue.

While he spreads the gluey sand
Frau S. squeezes out the glue.

While she zigzags glue on card
Felix cuts the cellophane.

While he cuts the plastic up
Marleen cuts the sheets of card.

While she cuts around the squares
Johannes sits and sorts the shells.

Puppet-Maker

Johannes has two puppets,
Rüdiger and Omegepta.

Rüdiger von Drachenblut is a kind of frog
made from blue socks and other scraps,
his polystyrene eyes
coloured green with highlighter.

Omegepta's female. She's a blond dog
with a dalmatian mask she sometimes wears.

Rüdiger and Omegepta
have appeared on youtube
speaking in the same monotone
as Johannes, or singing classic rock.

Name

my grandmother's name was Chris.
ach ja – Christl.

a chrism, christ with a lemon tongue.
turquoise water inside a glass
wörthersee water
a crystal you take in your pocket or carry
touching your neck

a pair of blue and glass eyes
from a black and white portrait

a ring of yellow hair
Chris
in your army green cap

Christl
a baby lying over a stream
or the picture of a baby

Es war einmal

I

A farmer was walking by a stream when he saw a basket had been left there. There was a baby, miraculously, asleep inside. Glücklich für das Kind, the soft, fine day; the slow wind didn't wake her.

II

They called her Christl, because she came like Christ in a mean way, out of doors, and was conceived like him, mysteriously.

III

The farmer had neighbours who, it was well-known, could not have children, and this was a great burden. The farmer's wife felt that God had laid a gift in her hands, and she was grateful for what she alone had the power to give away.

IV

She was adopted by these neighbours. Then when she was eight, Christl's first sister was born. Heidi, with hair all over her little skull. Then came Irmgard, Günther, the twins Roswitha and Anne-Marie, and Harry.

V

At 21 she worked in a canteen in green army uniform, serving meals to British soldiers after the war. First Frank hooked her waist and touched the bright yellow curl that emerged from her cap to rest on her cheek. One night, he stuck his dick in her. The other man came, and he wanted to take her to England and marry her, and Christl had nowhere else to bring the child, and she would not leave it by the river, so she crossed the sea.

now I'm a bit mad at me mam, never adopted me properly, why not?

ah that's what they said, she'll probably get some more children that's why she never had me adopted that's what they said

then afterwards after five years would you believe and she starts having kids then she had six! She was lucky she had me, helping her I mean

then she had Heidi, then nothing for five years, none for five years after that,
then she has Günther,
then she has Irmgard,
then she has TWINS!
then Harry was the youngest

I would have liked to have Werner adopted. They want to sort it out get your papers and everything

because when Hitler came to power and Austria joined up to Germany you had to have papers all of a sudden about this aryan thing and that

Villach

The Erlendorf house was grey; no one came to the door. A dark-green, electric-locked gate; thick tape on the mouth of the newspaper tube on the mailbox. Is that a surveillance camera? Small tubular box-eye at us, with its slow, red-dot pulse.

We cycled asphalt Radwegs by the Autobahn and under heavy bridges, by mineral-green streams and recycling plants. Then down gravel, scuffed paths that cut through trees and dark-green mountains, massive on either side. A clear, turquoise lake; graffiti; warm grassy air; spots of rain.

STOP 2: LUDWIG-WALTER STRAßE 20

Looking from the side the house was on, under the pink faded church, a car-show called WERNER. Next to that, a 24-hour casino and a netcafe; on a bus-stop, a women's underwear advert. Further along, by the crossing, SCHNITZELWELT.

At the point of the address itself, a dozen new apartment buildings in matte grey, nos 15–25 interchangeable, the handle at 20 a big plastic mitt-shape.

Werner, my uncle told the address where my grandmother lived to us over the phone; he added it was opposite a church 'with two onion domes'.

I wish she'd never told me

Somebody found me, they must have worked at the farmer's, in the country. Farmers brought me up till I was two then me mam went to this gasthaus and me father went there for a drink and somebody came in with a little baby.

The doctor said she couldn't have children and me mam loved children, she took me in her arms, lifted me up and I wouldn't let go
I put me arms right around her neck and I wouldn't let go
The woman said would you have her or something she said she'd have me

Well, laugh then! This is how she told me, me mother. I wish she'd never told me, and they'd adopted me properly and I'd have their name.

Somebody found me there just in time, if they hadn't found me I'd be dead. It's funny life when you think you get born, you weren't here before, then you die and it's just, you're not there anymore

Schloss Cumberland

I

Landespflege und Betreuungszentrum
it's a fake fairy castle
like disney lego

there's one bit that's old
curly locks on the door
white roses im Garten

goats who spoke to me loudly
and a hidden lake

II SCHREI

past the wall it's loud
down to the lake

pain of a man cries the day
in closed rooms

it recedes, but every few minutes
on cue returns

cries the lake
past the day it recedes

in closed loud
pain on the wall

cue the man
every few minutes

After the duke died, it was a museum
for a while, with swords and embroidery
done by the women. Then the nazis

shelled it out and made
a trainingszentrum for a year, then
a war hospital. Tuberculosis bodies whirled

in the decades. In 1979
they did it up. Red Ebensee marble,
grey marble from Villach.

Now there are six special beds
for patients who won't wake up, and a shed
to do knitting, woodwork, felting or painting.

there was this fellow

and there was this fellow running about with his back out and a big hole in his lungs

he must

everything just hung out, and there was no doctor. Everyone laying there like animals, laying about!

have been

I distinctly remember this soldier running about with his cap on

alright if he was

and they were all laying there on straw, like animals

running about

this fellow running about with a big hole in his back

with his back

and there was nobody there to help him no doctor they said

out!

1943–5 Ebensee

HAUPTEINGANG

The rest of the camp's
built over by houses;

only the calloused
grey gate remains.

White, brown, squares of yellow
houses, village tarmac.

Only the scab-grey gate remains
from what was built here

first, hidden by trees.

TUNNEL

In the base of the Seeberg
a cold hole.

20000 moved wood and rock
to hull it out.

Square-ribbed
corridor. Clicks

from the broken
light strip;

drips from the open-cut
mountain body.

you don't know what's true

I didn't know there were concentration camps, I knew they locked them up in a prison but I didn't think they did that. You don't know what's true, I only found out about the concentration camps when I came to England

in the pubs the gestapo listen and take you away, I thought they take you to ordinary prison not the concentration camps where they do this and that

I saw once they chucked all the furniture out of the window of a Jew's shop. There were lots of Jews there, people worked for them. We had a lot of Jews in Austria. In Villach nearly all the shops were Jewish

In and Out of Europe

In 2016, polling day,
I'm swimming in the Traunsee,
Oberösterreich.

In 1946, my grandmother came
to Britain, and spoke kein deutsch
to her children.

As a child she swam
in the Faakersee, Wörthersee,
River Gail;

I swam as a child
in the Eamont, Ullswater,
Cumbria.

There's a Schloss in the town
I'm living in, named for
my constituency:

'Cumberland, a lake-rich
county of England',
where I vote by proxy.

I'm not coming to a country

why did they let us come here then, to torture us!
write your travellers' cheques on this piece of paper
must have been a reason everyone got married after the war, they
supposed to be your enemy
and put that somewhere separate to your travellers' cheques
I didn't know they were short of housing and they bombed it in
so if someone nicks your travellers' cheques you've got this other
bit of paper
I'm not coming to a country they bombed all in, I never would
have come
get them from Thomas Cook
can't even get your own place, everybody had to live with some-
body
on the transalpino it's quite nice, you go all through Europe
I didn't come here to be rich or anything, but I expected a home
and you haven't seen Europe, so it's quite enjoyable

notes on climate change

The more I read on the subject, the more I find I need to know about economics, politics, geography and science. But these are areas I barely studied at school. I am trained to respond to texts: literature, music, the visual arts. Thankfully, I am equipped with the skills to scan and comprehend the main points of articles; this allows me better to understand, but not to do.

BLACKOUT

Coal/oil/gas needs to stay put, in the ground. Reduce emissions to zero.

What if a magician clapped his white-gloved hands and all the machines stopped their cranking and burring, mechanical arms stilled? Stage goes black. Combustion stops.

———

Then chaos; conflict; money wars; people with backyard generators running out to chop wood for fires

———

We could accept the proposition of some of the major religions that the self is nothing. We could let go of the self and allow it to dissolve. With this in mind, changes that are coming are nothing more than a great wave. We wait, death grows towards us and widens its embrace. We don't panic but are still, and it carries us away, at some time or another.

———

But the religions also teach us to save others, before thinking of our own death. Because the world is full of creatures
who did not play a part in this.

I skip the paragraph on extinction. Yes, so this will happen… 40% of species wiped out (mosquitoes remain, spreading malaria. I hardly ever see them anyway). Birds, a fox sometimes. In the country, sheep. If I want to look at reefs or pangolins I can always stream them.

———

If you're a victim of childhood obesity or an eating disorder, then you will have other things to think about.

———

Fred is thinking about how to make his day in the office stuck to the computer bearable. He's already stopped for lunch and snacked on a couple of Jaffa Cakes. He's meeting Sara after work; he'll also have to find time to pick up supper from the supermarket; for example, a salmon en croûte. He's going to download the game he wants now online while he should be working. If he's got the motivation to-morrow he should get to the gym before work. That'll make him feel good and closer to perfect; at least, closer to OK.

———

Even if your house has been flooded you have other things to con-sider, such as whether you should move, and also, what kind of new kitchen units you and your husband both like.

———

John thinks, when he gets back to England from travelling he'll buy a little second-hand car to run around in. Who are you to say he shouldn't have it?

THE SUBJECT

In general, times when we are able to find happiness correlate with omission of the subject. Most activities function perfectly well with-out its consideration. Outside work, we can even buy lunch out or a cake and coffee, go out for drinks, purchase a book or record. We can relax in a spa or book a plane ticket to a lesser-known European city, thereby providing a pleasant interruption to the routine and something new to photograph.

We can even grow fruit, keep chickens and bees, cook together and have sex. We can wander on mountains, draw or paint the colours and shapes we see around us, sing or join a band. We can learn languages, read about other cultures, or take on Proust. We can learn a skill, like knitting, papermaking or cake decoration. We can go camping, do a cycle trail. We can use the internet to share opinions and keep up to date. We can do this without remembering the subject. We can do most of these things without really thinking.

———

Actually, it crops up. In this part of Austria it crops up whitely, in the absence of snow. A 17-year-old boy told me of his ambition to be a ski instructor. He spends his holidays teaching on the slopes and is paid €200 a day. He loves skiing. But there are fewer and fewer instructors here. This winter was wetter, Christmas was wrong. At the February carnival, one float was painted with unsaid words like the silent victim of a strangling – *Wann wird es wieder richtiges Winter?*

———

In this small town, the elderly walk about over-hot in their antique furs and wool caps pinned with birds' feathers. Maybe a few days a winter, now, can Frau Stellinger put on her best sleek fur to go around town. She takes it off once she's reached the warm bank for her appointment.

On the dry road surface, some triangles of green
bottle glass flash yellow-white with bending rays.
Till rocks melt wi' the sun, my dear,
Till rocks melt.

silver white winters that melt into springs

The winter was a thick covering of snow between late november and early march. You lived in boots and overcoat, ate knödel and went skiing and tobogganing. Then the snow melted with the rising song of birds and the lifting of crocuses from the ground, and you knew it was spring. And spring was fresh, sunny and sometimes showery, so you knew when summer arrived when it got warm all the time. And once you put your coat away it was away for good, and you could swim in the lake every day. Then august would gather its humid shawl of leaves and flies and storms would shake us into autumn, when all of the green was eaten away or hidden, and it was time to cuddle together inside.

it's warm in december and can snow in april, rain may flood
through all the weeks in may and when it's hot, it's achingly
white hot heat and when it snows, it spits wet pellets then melts
on dark grey roads and there are
no more
clear winter days or autumn sunshine
just sticky long grass flying in a wet wind

Eisblumen

Ernst was the son of Ernst Konditorei and he had to take up the family business, though he did not like making cakes. He did not want to be inside a small kitchen rolling dough and piping rosettes when he could be in the fresh forest air. He had wanted to be a forester.

When he retired, his daughters were married and the shop closed. To make up for lost time, he woke at 3 a.m. each day and cycled to the hills, where he painted pictures. He had a pole fixed to the back of his bicycle where he taped the wet pictures to dry while he rode home. In winter the water on the pictures froze on the way down, and there were ice-flowers – Eisblumen – in them.

It used to be ever so hot in Austria,
not so hot now, the weather's changing, it's like in England.
When I came to England first the weather was really
warm and I thought it's warm in England nice here not so cold

because it's frosty in Austria
you get all flowers you can see out the window
you couldn't even see through because of all those ice flowers

get up in the morning freezing
get dressed straightaway make a fire
in the kitchen, we used to stay in the kitchen nice and warm there

then you boil the milk

he always had scrambled eggs and coffee
before he went to work,

I used to get the kids' breakfast ready. Haferflocken, oats cook it
then put it through a sieve, it's good stuff that, not like this
powder they have today.

Then we cooked our breakfast, I had to fetch the milk, always fetch
our own milk from the shop, sunday as well, then you boil the milk

kill all the germs, get a special can and boil it

Milk

Jessica has heard of the need to cut out dairy. Cows produce all that methane, that contributes to global warming.

But she still would like to have her tea and milk, coffee and milk, porridge made with milk; her children to have milk with their biscuits; roux sauce for the lasagne; pancakes occasionally and if she's up to making it, homemade ice cream.

She tries soya in a Tetra-Pak. It tastes bitter-healthy, like a plant stem, so thin and bitter it must be healthy.

Then she hears how rainforests are cleared to make room for soya, mainly for cattle feed to support the demand for meat (Jessica is already a vegetarian), but also for all these cartons people drink from (then throw away).

She switches to almond. The taste is butter-sweet, nutty-smooth, good in coffee especially with sugar.

Then her friend posts an aerial view of almond trees in California, hundreds of thousands of hectares of pink fluffy squares, pollinated by a million beehives disaffected by transportation annually there and the pesticides sucked up in the blossom; and the trillion gallons of water required to water these almonds, so they can be pulped and added to water, cartoned and shipped in milk to Jessica.

She tries rice. Surely here can be nothing wrong? The milk is sweet and thin; she imagines the delicate grains like splinters of shell poised on her tongue. But the paddies too take so much water to maintain. And all these cartons can't be good either, with their chewy layers of cardboard, foil and plastic covering, tough to recycle.

She decides to make her own. Buys a sack of oats and a small bag of hemp hearts (these are supposed to work well). Invests in a Vita-Magi-Supa-Mix and crunches the raw stuff up daily, the machine waking the household with its screaming, sharp-bladed purpose. Then the milk is foaming ready in a jug on the table, gadget unplugged, the electrical socket searing with heat.

lovely sausages

It was cheaper living in the country. Help on the farm and that, we didn't get money. You have your own pigs see, lovely sausages, all meat, never tasted anything as nice as that, bludwurst, not like this black pudding it's different

it was all rich but I never used to get fat, we used to eat all that. I don't know how they make it, beautiful, did you have some? Doesn't half taste lovely

it's rich and everything but people weren't that fat, weren't real thin but you worked harder then, always on the go I guess

British

I

Gainsborough – Reynolds – Constable –
Turner – empire – Tipu's tiger – a cup of tea
at the V&A – a light lunch – going to see
a show – things from the giftshop – neoclassical
lumps of sculpture – stuffed creatures – glass
eyes – café – audioguide – disabled access – ticket
holders only

II

We walked the grounds of a club in Putney: bridge
over pond, black geese and a kind of moorhen.
White wrought chairs for tea on the lawn, hard
and empty in pouring rain. Important to have
somewhere to retreat to in the city, with grass and
the river. Cane chairs in the conservatory. Soup,
butter, scones and salmon, please. Then I went to
the V&A and walked the stained glass aisle, which
faces the courtyard.

some people have tea

who'll have another cup of tea then go and make another cup of tea

cupper teas! Are we going to have our lunch or something, a bit of lemonade

she's got apple juice, would you like an apple juice

coffee in the morning, and coffee at night. Some people have tea, with lemon, and me father always had it with rum. In the winter we had rum in it. Keeps your body warm and that. Warm your body when you're cold, say you're freezing, in the winter you're not very warm you want a tea with rum. Me dad used to have some backed up in the winter, because it don't half warm your body and that, if it's really cold. That's what you do in Austria, some people have lemon, then you have lindenblüten tea, that's nice. Is this a linden-baum, out there? Looks like it, but it looks a bit dark, they're real light, the leaves

have a drop more tea you must be dry now
your tongue waggin', waggin' all afternoon

Austrian pastorals

i   the lake that's black in January.

ii   an a.m. running stream,
mineral off the Loser mountain.

iii   stepped out the car in Ratten
to a high clear air, „Die Post", tractor.

iv   Wolfsburg, for instance, was a zone of deaf white.

v   and the Villach canal, sprayed with weed.

vi   I lived on a hill in Kärnten
with piebald goats and barns.

vii   I'd go back to Tyrol's
whistling river,
I'd go to Vorarlberg's
houses made from wooden feathers.

viii   I climbed forests of mountains
and came out to insects, flowers,
razed trees, cattle.

where I walked the smooth roads
daily, passing chickens and the ridge
above the cemetery.

somewhere

I should've married in Austria
    they wouldn't be here then
If I hadn't worked for the English
    I'd be here
get a nice boy in Austria
    but I'd be somewhere else
life's made out for you
    how would you be here
I don't know how it works
    but be somewhere else?

Glossary

page

17	wohnung	apartment
	See	lake
	drei könige	three kings
18	Konditorei	cake shop
	Kaffee-Kuchen	coffee and cake
26	Eck	corner
27	*Wenn... beschieden*	if you still have a mother / thank God and be content / not everyone on this Earth / is granted such luck
	Internat... Verboten!	boarding school (entrance forbidden!)
30	fasching	carnival on the Tuesday before Lent
	schmankerlstube	snack bar
	bosner	type of sausage
	indianer	Native American
31	*was... Leben*	what can be more beautiful / than a little new life?
33	berufsschule	vocational college
35	schweinfleisch	pork
42	Es war einmal	once upon a time
	Glücklich... Kind	lucky for the child
44	Radwegs	cycle paths
	Autobahn	motorway
46	*Landespflege und Betreuungszentrum*	landscape management and care centre
49	Haupteingang	main entrance
51	Oberösterreich	Upper Austria
57	*Wann... Winter*	When will winter be right again?